Adopted Twice for
KIDS

Biblical Stories of Adoptions for Today's Adoptees

Written by Lyndy Stokes

Illustrated by Claire Williams

WestBow Press books may be ordered through booksellers or by contacting:

WestBow Press
A Division of Thomas Nelson & Zondervan
1663 Liberty Drive
Bloomington, IN 47403
www.westbowpress.com
1 (866) 928-1240

Interior Image Credit: Claire Williams

ISBN: 978-1-9736-7460-3 (sc)
ISBN: 978-1-9736-7461-0 (e)

Library of Congress Control Number: 2019913876

Print information available on the last page.

WestBow Press rev. date: 09/20/2019

WESTBOW
PRESS®
A DIVISION OF THOMAS NELSON
& ZONDERVAN

Dedicated to every adopted child. God loves you and has a special plan for your life. –LS

A New Home for Moses

God brings families together in different ways. In the Bible, God gives children the families they need. God loves all the little children very much.

When Moses was a baby, it was not safe for him to stay in his home. Moses' mother prayed and trusted God. God provided a way for Moses to be safe.

God delivered baby Moses to another loving mother. She brought Moses into her home and cared for him. She even asked Moses' first mom to help too!

God used Moses to save the Israelites from bad things.

Moses was very important to God.

You are very important to God too! He gave you a new home, and you also have two moms who love you very much!

Queen Esther

When Esther's parents died, she went to live with her cousin Mordecai. He took care of her and treated her like a daughter.

One day, the king decided he was going to look for a new wife. He invited all the young women to the castle.

Esther was chosen to be queen! But there was a bad guy working for the king, who wanted to hurt Esther's family. His name was Haman. But Esther had a plan.

Esther invited the king and Haman to a dinner. She told the king that Haman was planning to do mean things.

The king listened to Esther, and sent Haman away to punish him. Esther believed God would protect her family. And He did!

God helped Esther become queen, so she could help others.
God wants you to help others too!

A New Family for Ruth

Sometimes bad things happen, and people are left alone. Ruth decided to live with Naomi, and they became mother and daughter.

Naomi and Ruth were family because they loved each other. They were stronger together than they were apart.

One day, Ruth met Boaz. He took care of not only Ruth but Naomi too.

God used Ruth and Boaz, and after many, many years Jesus was born into their family. Jesus wants everyone to be part of His family.

Boaz + Ruth

Obed

Jesse

Jesus

David

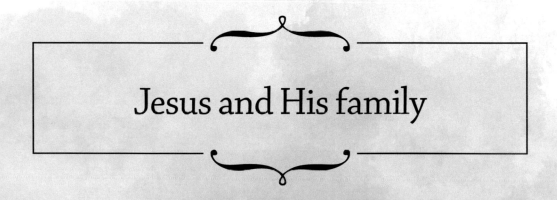

Jesus and His family

God had a very special plan for Mary. She was going to have a baby!

Mary and Joseph knew that God was in control. They were excited about Jesus coming!

Jesus is the Son of God, but Joseph took care of Jesus just like a son. He taught Him to walk and talk, and loved Jesus very much!

When Jesus grew up, He helped many people. He helped blind people see, He healed people who couldn't walk, and He took sickness away from sick people.

But the best thing Jesus did was loving us. He loved us so much. He became the only Way for us to go to Heaven.

Jesus loves you very much! He cares about you and gave you a wonderful family. Jesus adopted you into His family too!

"For I know the plans I have for you," declares the Lord, "plans to prosper you and not to harm you, plans to give you hope and a future." – Jeremiah 29:11